FEELINGS.....

(Poems)

FEELINGS.....
(Poems)

Dr. Amita Saxena
Professor
College of Fisheries
G.B. Pant University of Agriculture & Technology
Pantnagar – 263 145, India

2011
REGENCY PUBLICATIONS
Delhi - 110 002

ISBN 81-89233-66-1
ISBN 978-81-89233-662

Published by : **REGENCY PUBLICATIONS**
(*Division of Daya Publishing House*)
4760-61/23, Ansari Road, Darya Ganj,
New Delhi - 110 002
Phone: 23245578, 23244987
Fax: (011) 23260116
e-mail : info@regency-books.com
website : www.dayabooks.com
website : www.regencybooks.com

Laser Typesetting : **Classic Computer Services**
Delhi - 110 035

Printed at : **Chawla Offset Printers**
Delhi - 110 052

PRINTED IN INDIA

Contents

Plant

Plant, you are small,
But well shaped and shady,
The stalk is bent,
The apex is hanging,
Do you shameful and...
Don't know your beauty and grace
Or so kind and polite.....
Inspite of your grace.....
The beautifully coloured flowers,
Dark green shady leave, snowy fume
And sensational sweet perfume,
Nature teaching to all,
Things preaching to all,
Have a look at plant,
Learn the lesson of greatness at a glance.

Sorrow

Sorrow and happiness are intervened
Both are compulsory for life, no one recovered
In the absence of one
No one can find the importance of another,
If all is going smooth,
Nothing to be smooth,
Smoothness lost, its smoothness,
Life will become dull,
It is only sorrow, not to borrow,
Do not burrow, it is arrow,
That provide strength,
Candid courage for life
The courage for strength
And provide new wave to life
New wave will clear the truthful tree,
meaning of life
Not long, for a while,
Bear sorrow cheerfully,

Live the life cheerfully,

No sorrow, no tomorrow,

Tomorrow never comes,

Today, to time, to this movement.

There is no sorrow

This is challenge time

A change time for happiness

Do great in this change time for happiness.

Strange Behaviour

Dog's eye reflected on me,
Jumping, hopping, humming together,
Coming going, leaping, tracking,
Waiting on hind legs,
Showing soul through touch,
Sat on, set up literally hand in hand
Showed Friendliness
Strange, Ready to Run hand in hand
Strange gesture, posture pity pleasant,
Move Special shapes, welcome beloved and guest.

God

God is great,
God made you,
So, you are great,
See, yourself,
You will find a God ....
Who will, not that,
What you are thinking,
Like an idol?
But an ideal!
Whom you are expecting?
Who will teach you?
All what you are wanting?
That will perfect you.....
You will, not be, wanting
You will say
God is great
Who made you
This way great.

Human

All plants are living organisms,
Animals the minute, one amoeba is,
Also a living organism,
Every plant and animal doing all they,
Why grace is within all way,
Why not in human being,
Artificiality in human being,
The highly evolved become primitive,
Not primitive, determinitive
Become animal,
Away from confusion,
Animals are better,
They live better,
But the man,
Loss his goodness for better.
Great problem, cater poison
To be better
Its not bad, bitter,

But do better make better,
And to become best of all,
It will become best of all,
Life is nothing, more than all,
It is only the best of all.
Best human, in best of all
Creatures.

Life

Life is full of life,
See the life with life,
You will find a life in life,
An eye to life
Provide, a way to life,
For you and all.
Life, Life and Life
Grateful God
Give me life.

Old Man

Life is like a flower,
It is a bead when you, young,
Gives ambition and sense of beauty,
Gives pleasures to young and duty,
The colourful vision attracts to all,
Butterfly comes fruits are formed,
Fruits are beneficial to all
As the old experienced person,
Beneficial to all

Calmness

Nature is natural,
May man of earth,
The Volcano brust,
Life disturbed,
May be, by man or earth,
Volcano is checked,
Internal is disturbed,
To check the disturbance,
Volcano is must,
One is to be disturbed, Internal or external
It should be external,
So internal will be calm,
Down to earth,
Live in nature's peace

Rains

Rains are falling from sky
Saying Bye Bye to sky,
Tears are falling from eye,
Breaking the bridges of my eye,
Rains are cleaning the sky,
Tears are cleaning my eye,
Rains drips making spectrum
My tears also making spectrum
But rains are happy, cause happiness,
But I am not happy not cause happiness
Rain drops are better useful,
My salty tears are useless
Rains are cleaning the sky plants tree, dust and earth
But my tears cleaning only my thick thrust of eyes.

Moon

Night is dark
Sky is dark
Stars hide
Moon hide
Clouds cover, star, moon
A splash of height, light
Show the Moon, slight
Give the hope, to, brightness
Waiting.......
When clouds vanish
Make me relish.

Beauty

Girl is so beautiful
Her eyes are beautiful
Nose is sharping all the mountain
Lips are thin but prouting, fountain
Voice is haunting,
She is chanting,
Life is wanting,
Wants of beauty,
Lacks of duty,
Beauty is duty,
And dutiful is beautiful.

Anoid Bud

Today, Life
Whole world
Looks ....
So, strange, ...
Seems
To be, asking my name?
Who were welcoming?
Some time before ....
Bestow blessings, beautifully bright blushing buds,
On me, while walking
Now, I am alone with my own memories
I made indelible marks
Were not these your words?
I and you, Both are same
Why vision so strange?

Why so

Every one born on earth,
In a similar way,
Why to be strange with some?
Not with other!
Those not come to your range......
Logic fails, As all, one out of range,
Things are same, demands are same,
Survival for the same,
It is difficult to understand,
This discrimination game,
Who so?.......

Maina

I was, driving my car,
Bird maina running to far,
To cross the road,
Stop, and run, not fly
Bird way thought, if danger I will fly
I slowed the car to make her successful,
Thought move on road not to fly,
When she crossed the road completely,
She flied fully with wonderful wings spreadly,
It was her attempt to do unusual,
Or to chase for patience high mutual
When pretty play fire fly
Animal see the transparently, free and enjoy
Gives me happiness
Why terror is created by human
Wait and watch the play,
See the Nature's way to Gay.

Gain

I and you live between the grinding stone,
When they move, crush to one
Pick us to fate,
Where is the gate?
Gate is you, bring out of you,
I with you, we will do
Fate is you, you are you,
And never say,
You and I Live
Between the grinding stone
Stoney are always gainful
Never feel painful,
Through their hardness,
Thoroughness of life.

Pain

Be painful,
Know it why?
Pain is sensitivity
Pain is life,
Peaks, reach to tender emotions
No one know,
What is pain,
You will never in loss,
Always in gain,
Gain to you and all,
See the pain once again,
Then know the matter of gain,
Painful is a gainful life,
You will get a height,
Which is white,
White is colourful,
Make your life colourful,
Pain enhance the depth,
Penetrate the ocean depth.

Creation

Life is brief,
Full of grief,
Never grieved,
As miseries are unreal,
Deceptive thoughts
Only deceptive thoughts,
Above the thoughts,
Bring out yourself
Above these thoughts,
Hearts will open, you will find,
Mind will open, an open mind,
An open heart
Both will give renunciation
Both will give you a recreation
That will be a creation
And finally renunciation

Lime Light

When I see light ......
Who, made it world bright
Are you right? See it again .....
You find a bright,
Penetration, piercing plight
But world ....
Oh! Unaware of the glory of His light,
Use, use, use ....
Never refuse ....
You are serving, never tiring
Oh! You are great .....
Never look back, any crate,
Only go on doing, doing, doing,
Light is with you,
Only with you,
Only for you,
This is My light
Make you in Lime light

Cautions

Life of poor or a rich,
Pass or failure full of caution,
Cautions, about self and others,
When we alone or together,
A deed, a Carelessness,
Cause you dispairness,
People will say you are damn
Why people, call you damn
Why not, you cautious
Which is essential for both.

Land

Where is our native land,
The birth land,
Is it a land mark?
Or a trade mark?
On me on my head
Speaking colour, eyes, nose, hair,
Here and there but fair .....
Seeking land to live,
What to give?
No, no, I, I ....
Seeking land, our Native land.
To live and die.

Attraction

Black alert, eyes, look lively
Upward cheeks, high, high cheek bones,
Rosy lips pearl teeth inside as,
Show inside, the rosy petals, smiling mantras
Love, respect, devotion, adoration
What will make me cherished combination?
Creating
Goodwill peace altogether
Yet roaming, unware of her
Aware of all, who is there?
Who is she?
Godess Laxmi,
Sheding gold coins,
On my way to knowledge.

You My Sun

You are my perceptual cognition
Increasing memory, high recognition
By hearing you, I gained rational knowledge
The place, time for me are oriented by you
You are the Sun
I am like a Satellite
I am dead
Without you
My direct knowledge from you,
The only fascinating fire
Come to me, give to me,
All from you
Give me perfection,
Love and devotion,
You.......my Sun!

Realization

The passions, desires,
Emotions, and infatuations,
Are depositing on my soul,
I found ....
I deprieved of knowledge of you,
Losing my identity, my originality,
Where was I ?
What I do ?
Nothing else?
I don't know
I really lost, my vital powers,
.........Regain it .... How's? ......
Check the passions, sentiments
They cause you, shatters,
Inflow of unnecessary matter,
Realise yourself, remove all layers of wasteful
Now, I solved and regained identity
And thoughts came naturally
To its own originality.

Tootache

My tooth molor polished,
  shined
Enamel,
Eaten by my carelessness,
Make it, black cavity,
Like our gravity
Pain! oh! severe pain,
Unbearable, untolerable pain
Escaped from limit, creating
Crying, shouting, shievering legs
Stability lost
Things they lost,
Lost forever
Why not through it out,
Not ready even for filling,
World's drilling
Straight way extraction and finally extracted out
Society rooted out
My conscious awaked and
I got the way of living,
Careful, caring, pleasuring, giving
Otherwise ....
Society rooted out,
World, old not maintained
  man out.

Summer Night

Summer Sun, settle down
Dark night at nine O' clock,
The haunting small of Chrysanthemum,
Smoothing winds after sunny heat strokes
Clean, lonely street with neon bulbs,
The bloomy scraps..............
The rich leaved green tree touching, sky.....
Purifying environment even my ideas, my brain
A pleasurable relied to mental, mental electrically
Message of purity sanctity and sanity,
The fragrance of you happiness and gaiety,
Lovely breeze after a long - long..........
...................Striking heat strokes,
Sandy summary strokes,
Cool, calm, comfortable at night

Evil Chooses Wisdom

Oh! evil leave me,
You are fertile,
Breeds hatred, malice and contempt's,
All unvirtuous deeds,
I am not in needs
Leave me barren,
You cause all calamities
Especially degrading brown in my own
Humiliation, putting me down,
Is something worsen like it,
No................oh!   No!
Evil responded, be silent, inoffensive
Kill me with silence, love
Make me sterile, inactive and ineffective
I asked Are you saying to evil
The evil saying to
————————Evil says————————
I like wisdom - wisdom, where? when? why?
All wisdom only wisdom, Always win
Advise, Use wisdom.

Death

The broad wide dark, studded starry sky,
When, my body lie on pyre,
Lit by fire, the fire from hill,
Bell rung at the time of funeral, with a song
Burnt my wasteful, changeable body,
Liberating the eternal soul to survey the earth,
Visiting the earth by soul, An achievement,
Because I did goody, my soul surveyed gladly
And I died gladly,
My soul was happy and gay,
As was in eternal home way

Train Compartment

At once we rushed some crushed in
Train........... compartment
Soon see....... out,
Whistling of train, leaving behind plateform
People, places, pillars, plants and popcorn, pepsi,
Houses go wheeling back, too much juicy, trepsi,
Moving the background, up down electric wire,
Replaced by new place, plants, people, pilla
You also replace by new
Life you are moving, life new,
Every thing is stable,
But life is moving.

Misguided

Why your shape, spoiled, distorted face
Eyes drooping, features displaced,
Tongue discharge saliva again, and again
Uncontrolled evil, ill words and deeds
Poisoned breath, inspired and expired,
Is it a ride? Where? we go?
Or mere innocence or misguidance to think,
Body and nature, to wink
Is it good for a creature? Dull, No!
Sparkling in eyes stiffed necks sweetness
All appeared strong But ......
All seems, May be misguided ....
All your visions ....spoiled
Misguided by external force,
Miscarry the eternal essence.

Your Image

The memory in winter,
Of you ....
Forget all, senses of cold, forced,
Immediately, get up and moved,
The smoky mist mid night ....
Oh! Joggy foggy weather, your image,
I shouted, walked, reached ridge,
Got only the withered leaves, causing voice
My breath with smoke, intermingled with fog invoice
Like you with your chanting beauty,
Imagination, truth, reality all in you cuty,
All comes true with your arrival,
It is the cause of my survival!

Ingratitude

Winter wind blows so fiercely,
Penetrating the heart and mind piercely,
But not so unkind, So painful?
As one's ingratitude!
Oh wind you are impersonal, invisible,
You should not be blamed for, heart hurt,
How, I forget the ungrateful, plight,
Who is piercing at every sight?
With a severe pain,
Distorting my shape, my way,
More than freezer, winter, water
Freeze the Earth, Sun, Sky, Mentor.

Hollow Life

Adversities, embitter my life,
The leaf, flower, butterflies silent,
I cannot hear chirping birds,
All emotions crushed and beaten down,
Sparkling Sun teasing me,
Heart sad, sinks full of grief,
Only tear can express my belief,
How can I say my toughest brief
The silent voice of my hollow life,
Eating my soul, scratching by knief.

Friends Death

O! Death Oh! God
On whose step I approach you
Whom I complaint,
I loss of my grasp like greasy grass,
This shaking my internal,
When I saw your external,
Why you snatched my friend,
When the glory of his prime
I saw your glory this time.

Oh! God!

Oh! no, it is more than enough,
For me the world is rough,
Never with any one, friend or foe,
Joys of the days, gone by ways
Not, come back to me, any more,
The time, events objects delighted us when we more,
Together will cause grief to me
All world, life has changed totally, me,
World remain the same, to me
But my depth, height intensity everything lost
Oh world! Oh! God its too much to me.

Lost Life

The storm of grief rising to raise long,
Palpating the heart like sea, heart is full, silent tongue.
A cheer and merriment for doctor and observer,
Feeling a patient or object
But heart beat increasing
As memory in mind miserably increasing,
The life of my friend never comes back,
Which is lost once can never be recalled, back
Block the track,
No body can come back,
No one can, left this, eternal track.

Utilize Time

All the flowers, beautiful charming today,
Will be with tomorrow,
The butterflies never fly,
On deadly flower beak,
Sun reached to its peak
Will set down in the evening,
Food destroyed after certain time,
All things are subject, to decay,
The brightest thing, in briefest way,
Time not utilize at its prime,
Causing the worst life, self crime
It is fleeting, invariably,
Not waiting for anyone inquisitively.

Childhood

High tide of sea,
The divine innocence of a child,
Not hear the thunder, roaring sound,
Of waves ....
Makes no difference in playing with inner bliss,
But adult enjoy or sad ....
As his mood ....
Lovely sights and sounds stir soul,
The child play and enjoy with innerbliss,
Free from all passions and sorrow,
Unaware of tomorrow.

Sunny

Oh daisy flower sunny,
Regulating by Sun with gold shine,
Silvery light closing you and mine,
Night comes you and me lulled to sleep
With a hope, Sun rises
And bright us, with fresh rays
Thus, relieving us the wariness weariness of day,
Sun shines, day comes, shores
Brings us closer than ever before,
It happens every day,
But we wait for every, new day.

Truth

House is not built without basement,
Person is not built without truthment,
Without truth no body can serve,
Service of truth is selflessness nerve,
It is realization of truth,
A stable happiness,
By leaving behind false and lasting objects,
All are like continuous flow of water,
Float over it, with truth
And realize the truth, love the truth.

Money Money

Money, Money, Money
My honey, you are far, Jeney
Your joy, fraud, deceptive
Illusion, hallucination, hypersensation,
Raising hair flying over,
Nothing for ever,
But the day you come,
All world come under my feet,
My nuptial flights, lose the light,
More darker dark sky with wisdom bright,
Enlightened sight with money, alright,
That above the boredom money, plight,
You cheat, cheap money, money, money, might.

Mountain

The wide, most mountain range,
Broad, high touching sky,
As ambition of genius
Unusually rich in flora and fauna,
Unaware of man's touch,
For variant climate and habitat,
Appealing me straight and specific,
The diversity of nature,
Unhindered by its creature,
Naturally balancing and causing goodwill
Necessary pleasure will,
The treasure, to all,
Look at, know and enjoy,
Them without wall,
This is Nature's call.

Waiting Us

Waiting us, for a bus, there was rush,
Chances to crush,
Running men and women, children hush !
Waiting for bus ....
Standing us.........
Clouds showering, bowering........
Fearing us, got the bus, lowering.........
Gem packed bus, seating, sitting us,
Sweating us, inside, outside bus,
Glasses shut, wiper set,
Escaping us, wetting us,
By water, pure or saline,
We were wet it was time to wet,
Waiting us, waiting us.
For a city bus.

Directionless

One direction desire.......
Put me into the fire,
Destroy the ability,
Forced to heir,
And I suffered,
Aexial, Amnesia
Aphasia, dementia
Misleading me, loosing me
Sometimes dipsomania and
Then kleptomania
Mad me, my, shattered fate
Now way, gate
In a hypochondria
At waste dog, cheap laugh
Cause me pig headed dough,
Move all around!
Without direction!
Without ground!

Thrilled

Heart throbbed, I thrilled,
Seeing the weather, cloudy,
I shouted loudly.......
I ran ....
It will, rain, rain, rain?
Yaah, It rains!
Round drops in a sow, straight from sky
Shading the sky,
Like a pearl wreath,
Clearing the breath
You, me and she, thrilled, enjoyed whole heartedly,
Water, pure water depositely,
Pond, ditches, lake & rivers rich
Fish migrated, searching breeding ground,
Dancing peacock in dense forest, in heart background
Long thirsty papiha pee..h, pee..h, pee...
Taking drop by drop, ha..h..h..h....ha! ha!
All a lively pleasure, my heart throbbed to..to
All this glamour ....
I thrilled with joy to catch, touch sky, cloud
It rains, when it rains,
Ah........ It rains!

Who is

Who is ?
Pretty good at reporting,
Fairly well at noting,
Statue at painting,
Heavenly at dreaming,
Pleasuring at touching,
Leaving behind at racing,
Alluring when relating,
Fascinating at seeking,
Smiling at facing,
Who is ....
Waiting! ....!
Waiting to know.

Novoice

Novoice me
Dottered, viper oh! no,
Vixen ha ha........
Called recalled, echoed..........
Remained remise, will remembered,
Silent heart, silent mind,
Chattered tongue being kind,
Refined enjoyment believing epicure
No way to secure,
Alone me, novoice me,
Wakened conscious, every one cautious,
Silent heart, silent mind,
Silent tongue, shattered wicked,
Scattered silence, novoice me,
Scattered silence,
Novoice all!

Exonerated

Every body killed,
I was lived exonerated,
From fearing, loosing,
Elephant stepped gingerly on my chest
Thou, producing mirth, trapeze, test,
Searching you, waking you
As swinging bar through swinging you,
Same subject, object twinkling,
When Nights, will mine, days will mine
Every body killed I will live exonerated?
For what, for whom?

Collecting Straws

Collecting straws, fibre,
Beak grip starts, vibre,
Searching place, seeking home,
Safe, shelter secure,
Got the place, an open space,
Above the canopy face,
Making nest weaving, knitting,
Grateful, beak, helping great
Laying eggs, protecting caring
Wait to hatch ....
Emerging new, feeding few
Teaching flight, future fall bright
Doing same, collecting straw tight
Repeating repeating, teaching all
Weave, knit, protect care to all.

Nothing to Reach

A day, way, Sunday, gateway,
Both guy go there see there,
Stopped see, sea,
Moving waving raving craving, catching,
Wave, drip by drip, hut to mouth but drop,
No crop on earth but sea crop worth,
Going deep animal creep, in a sleep,
Catching feather urchin, horse, lily in a wily,
Fathom reach nothing to beach,
Wetted cloth with a doth,
Came back to beach nothing to reach,
A day, way, Sunday, gateway,
It is not beyond your reach.

He (GOD)

Who made flower colourful?
Who made buds beautiful?
Enquiring it! forest, garden wishful
Who gave boon of spring?
Who brought river to earth?
Who taught dance to peacock,
Who blessed night angle with sweet voice,
Enquiring it! whom, who?
He, He, He, Thy God He.........
You see the dream of He!..............
Forgetting He? No.........No.........he....he....he
Awake! and recognize, He!
He is every where,
He is in every breath and beat
He is.........only He
Who live with all
Who live in all.

Memory

Memory creeping, through mind
Like wave of storm of bay,
These were no force to bind
Reached to heart……Gay
Stretched the heart away my body
Puzzled me, my soul goody
Why I am here, make my vision shady
Illusion, lost me my soul say
I have no goal to way.

Real Need

Narrow brain, all are vain,
Stopped train, on pain,
Rushed passengers, out, in
Like us live, died in,
Some crushed, die in,
Like plant die in,
Dispersed seeds,
Died when lived, lived when died
Some narrow negatives die in open space,
Now allow positives to open pace
Life die without deed,
Lie victim of others greed
It is real need!
They live in their own creed.

My Sister

My sister, weeping loudly,
As sky weeping cloudly,
No can make happy her,
As she lost herself, irrepairable loss,
Choking throat, suppressed voice,
Only left, expression of tears ....
Forgot all what she wears?
Living as dead, moving as dead!
Without hope, any chance,
Fate caused her not to dance
Live within her tears.........
As an amoeba, straw in sea.

Leisure

Civilization developed busier as,
Leisure decreased, demand unceased,
Evolved us,
Going back to primitive stage
As uncivilized us,
Doing same, wearing same, eating same,
As we are in leisure .....
Away from smoking, back biting,
Tearing, spoiling reputation,
Enjoy as our ancestors,
Without fear
Civilized us in uncivilized, discipline
Civilized way.

A Girl

A girl passing through a street,
Every one walking on feet....as she,
Every, each eye at stir
Without any fear
Commenting and remarking
She is charming and enchanting
Replying the whistling and singing
The girl was smiling without lowered eyes
Inaudible voices.....
Confirming to be these in their affair
Everyone laughed and happy fair,
Every one following her.......
She reached her destination, said with smile
Come inside,
Ordered, arrest all, she was empowered
Empower the women
If you want real progress,
Development of India.

My Result

I opened the newspaper with trembling hands,
Oh! to what did I read! my nervous hands!
My name in block letters with photograph, days
All appreciating in their own ways,
Prouded me, my work, accorded recognition
Lots of felicitations leading celebration
Thank you, thank you, God! No one else, only you
You are the only one who make me happy in this ocean.
Recognised, Fresh and green in world sea.

Desire

A desire to achieve something,
Might be that is fame,
An aura of greatness around fame,
A glamour, sense of superiority,
Nothing like that, that is fame,
Breaking records, growing nails, longest kiss,
All for fame, yes, is that the fame?
A very fragile thing, takes long time to aquire,
Lose very easily within a seconds,
Desire, remains the same,
Never ending, increasing, always increasing.

Examination

Examination an integral part of education,
Test of intelligence and ability,
Judgement of knowledge,
All are reading, guessing, anticipating,
Waking, thirsty, hungry all over right!
I cannot sleep whole night,
Perhaps chances are bright!
Some are suffering from fever,
Examination extra fever, yes, your viral fever,
Taking drugs, goes to hall,
Read the paper write the answers
Comes out with holistic harmony on face,
Examinations over, temperature down,
Next is the enjoyment plan.
Oh exam! Finish soon for next plan.

We Don't Know

We are one,
But as I see the world,
We are none,
In search of one,
We agree with none
Having both qualities worldly & spiritually,
Still think, we are none,
World is away from us, we are away from world,
Why?
Who knows it?
No, only our answer
Yes, we know only, we don't know!

Loneliness

In this mighty world,
I am alone, lone long live,
Alone in ship;
Although it can accommodate many,
Prepared to raft,
Pick me to top of sky,
Source,
Some one frawn on my,
Rainbow flight,
I put them tight,
My healthy, wealthy glow,
See, heaven's bliss bright blow
My fear sys screamed to,
Strength of joys,
Some other lonely guys,
I came to earth, alone
I go from here, alone
But make the rainbow on,
An up the rainbow, crown,
Change, vision to facts,
Celebrate life as and when
you can acts.

Soul Mate

When I entered my heart saw you,
I found it is difficult,
When I stand you ask the same,
Both were caught by name,
Visualizing each other fame,
But what was the God's game,
Silence broken by shy shimming,
I could not recognize, The gate,
Reply came by heart I am soul mate
Lost in virtual rate, gate or fate
Impression came in eye to recognize
He is he, I could not recognize,
Seeing the eye hair and forehead,
Kissing the eye and forehead
Keeping the eye deep taking the sleep,
He is he, I could not recognize,
He showed the oldest, constructed, newly way,
Recognize duly daily say,
Eyes, hair, body, hand and soul,
Soul sees soul springs,
Soul left its soul with full swing,
Soul searching soul several says
Eyes enters eye eternal every ways
Wake up come up where they go, for ever,
For you, your ways.

Silence

The balls are moving round and round
Giving the message with sparkle, fond,
Saying all the history with unhearable sound,
Things are quite understandable,
But not understood
Every thing is known but unknown, could
Seedlings are there but ungrown would
Simplest the truth becomes mistry
It is the deep silence, wakes history.

Death

I was you corpse in red blanket
Your warm ways glaze, told your secrets
I touched you with my total endeavors
Your eyes, nose, lips, body wants to tell something
With full flowery favours,
With pink tinched glow, enhanced beauty blow
When I removed the blanket from your face
You smiled with grace
I removed your cloth and raised your head
You gave soften support
You were soft after a bath
Your were warm in cold
You dressed in sarees hath
Your soul swarmed, surrounding shells
You called "I am read to go" spread scents.
As usual we attend her call with tears tears
Take her to God's place and ask to give her
a good body
Tears on pyre, God grace her flesh, bones melted
Forever, for a new good body
For creation of new goals, new desires
with fresh soul.

On My Sister Death

My sister breathe to last,
Her soul, left me so fast,
I lie with her
She lies on my soul
From the last corridor of my memory
She cried, crippled crew crooked cause
Consciously seeing the hopeless us/world
Hopeful us/world
Give the developed science
Medicines failed, Apparatus changed,
Mighty Lord Hanuman was called
Lord Hanuman came, against swining death
Lord Hanuman rescued but not for a long length
With permission of Lord Hanuman,
  Yamraj took the soul away
Yamraj was in a pearl studed white cloth
On white broad bird flyer plane charriot

My sister exclaimed oh! My God,
See God is here, (He is God)
Yam, replied
My dear saint lady, I am not the God Lord Vishnu
I am Yamraj, No one else
I take you to Divine world, She said, Yes.
Sister soul said to us
Do not cry, Do not say, anything to me
You all live long, happily
I am going to Divine destiny
My place is decided there,
God placed me there,
Neither you are alone,
Nor I am alone,
For you, I am no more
I received flowers both ways
You flow flowered funeral ways
God give green gorgeous gainful garden

Bone flower when mixed with Ganges
Bestow blessings biggest blue be of heaven
My sister bowed before God
Almighty took me on highest, abode
She burned without cry
Tears came to cease fiery
This was the only destination
Although life is full of fascination.

Couple of Birds

A couple of birds
Communities of birds
Sit on wire
Waiting for fire
Friends to come
Crossing for some
Dating for some
Mating for one
We all move together, routine together
Let the sun rise
Love fly the wise
Long day of summer
Long way warmer
Morning evening
Sit on wire
A couple of birds

Fun

My tree taking to thou
Where were walls?
We wait, windy wipes
Whole night we were alone
You slept alone
Away
All my leaves burn on sun
Just feel fun
Jack jump joy jiggle to enjoy
All are fumes fragrance
Eternity evolve entire essential essence
You said
Join! just feel fun
See me what I do
We feel my green touch
You feel fun
We are not touch me not

You touch, we hard our knot

You cut sap sweeps

We fire for you

Just fun for you

My roots in soil

Your roots in vial

You spread in air

I spread when

As just for fun

Nothing give to me and fellow.

You

My entire world for you
We feel fun for you
But you!
Just feel fun!
Change change chain
Witting witting
Water water
See me not only for fun
Shelter me, Grow me
Shelter same shadow singing swallow
Swing air resting creatures
Giving miniatures
Not for fun, Not for fun.

Ways

I posed you different ways
I caused you different days
Name and fame impressed upon I
Nomination of you expressed upon you
Say you the truth teach you
Stupendous locations staged preach you
I think they all teach you
I think withering wilting you
When there is polishing
When you lose locks
All through the docks
I am levelling the polish.

Think

Conspirator thinks for conspiracy
Leader feel leadership
Bird enjoy to fly high
Fish goes to dive deep
I want lift multi direction
Creation and suggestion
Multi directional progression
Without any prohibition.

Feelings

You are swimming with me
You are flying with me
When I go deep in ocean
When I do high in cloud ocean
You see only my glimpse not me
You go back and lost me
When I search you
You torch me
You completely focused one
You drift all the directions for me
I rotated for you
I centered for you
With lightening divergent rays
Which convergent all at you
Starting swimming with deep
Seeking silky soften peep.